YOUR KNOWLEDGE HAS VALUE

Irina Giertz

Henry James and the American Realism

GRIN Publishing

Bibliographic information published by the German National Library:

The German National Library lists this publication in the National Bibliography; detailed bibliographic data are available on the Internet at http://dnb.dnb.de .

Imprint:

Copyright © 2005 GRIN Verlag GmbH
Print and binding: Books on Demand GmbH, Norderstedt Germany
ISBN: 978-3-656-85135-6

This book at GRIN:

http://www.grin.com/en/e-book/285212/henry-james-and-the-american-realism

GRIN - Your knowledge has value

Since its foundation in 1998, GRIN has specialized in publishing academic texts by students, college teachers and other academics as e-book and printed book. The website www.grin.com is an ideal platform for presenting term papers, final papers, scientific essays, dissertations and specialist books.

Visit us on the internet:

http://www.grin.com/

http://www.facebook.com/grincom

http://www.twitter.com/grin_com

Henry James – American Realism

Henry James (1843-1916)

Daisy Miller (1879)

The Portrait of a Lady (1881)

The Art of Fiction (1884)

Brooksmith (1891)

The Turn of the Screw (1898)

The Wings of the Dove (1902)

The Beast in the Jungle (1903)

The Middle Years (1914-1917)

References:

The Cambridge Companion to American Realism and Naturalism. 1995. Donald Pizer (ed.).

Amerikanische Literaturgeschichte. 1997. Hubert Zapf (ed.).

1. American Realism

    1.1. Problems of terminology

    1.2. Reasons for emergence

    1.3. Distinction from Naturalism and American Renaissance

2. Typical realism novel (The Portrait of a Lady)

    2.1. Characteristics of the American realism novel

2.2. Thematic and formal features of *The Portrait*

2.3. *Daisy Miller* – a study of the female protagonist

3. Sophistication of the realism novel (The Wings of the Dove).

    3.1. Focus on the characters' consciousness

    3.2. Contradiction – a melodramatic story and an evasive text

    3.3. Limits of objective representation

4. Elaboration of (American) realism novel

    4.1. Theory of literature in *The Art of Fiction*

    4.2. Further improvements - *Prefaces* to the New York Edition (1908)

American Realism

Problems of terminology:

1. literary and philosophical usages of the term Realism are distinct

2. realism refers not to the objective depiction of the reality but to the reality effect, something which is agreed upon as true or real

3. American and European periods of Realism do not coincide (European earlier R 1850-1880 N, American 1870-1880's R and 1890's N) and have different backgrounds (events, ideologies)

4. in the American literature R and N are clearly distinguished (Howells/James R, Norris/Dreiser N), in Europe often interchangeable

Reasons for emergence of American R:

– rapid industrialisation and urbanisation after the Civil War which ended in victory for

Northern capitalism (the Gilded Age 1865-1900 – ironic name given by Mark Twain due to unbridled materialism of the after war outburst of capitalism)

- revision of literature in the wake of the universal progress in all spheres (social, material, intellectual): the writer has to reject the romantic material and methods of the earlier fiction which was based on limited knowledge, in favour of a realistic aesthetics which demanded that the subject matter of contemporary life should be objectively depicted

- turn from sentimentalism to science which appeared to teach objectivity (see the world in its true light): Darwin *On the Origin of Species* 1859, *The Decent of Man* 1871

- turn to current affairs in novels due to the Civil War; major movements of the 2nd half of the 19th century: slaves, women, immigrants

- the promise of romantic democracy to settle all wrong matters right failed, increase of bureaucracy and corruption, ensuing distrust in the ruling elites

Literary Naturalism derives mainly from a biological model, its origin owes much to Darwin and his theory of evolution.

Zola *The Experimental Novel* 1880: novelist = scientist, observing nature and social data, rejecting supernatural explanations of the physical world, depicting nature and human experience as a deterministic and mechanistic process; reality can be explained by natural laws presented in scientific terms; two images of man: 1. the man of our future (H.G. Wells *The Invisible Man*) and 2. the degenerated man (*The Island of Dr. Moreau*). The new character of the naturalist novel is confronted with extreme situations which bring the irrational part of a person (impulses, instincts) to the surface.

Stephen Crane *The Red Badge of Courage* (1895)

Kate Chopin *The Awakening* (1899)

Frank Norris *McTeague* (1899)

Theodore Dreiser *Sister Carrie* (1901)

Jack London *The Call of The Wild* (1903)

Edith Warthon *The Age of Innocence* (1920)

Howells and James have often been regarded as cofounders of realism in the USA. Howells regarded the work of James as "character-painting", "a matter of painting what he sees", thus making its realistic quality slightly doubtful, describing James as a romancer. What his favourite character, Isabel Archer, says of personal identity ("Nothing that belongs to me is any measure of me; on the contrary, it's a limit, a barrier, and a perfectly arbitrary one.") is reminiscent of American Transcendentalism: the issue of free will vs. determinism.

Transcendentalism was the philosophy behind **"American Renaissance"** (1830's – 1860's) which usually describes a height of the American literature. New American literature was finally recognised in the world and, on the other hand, it displayed distinctive qualities of the American culture and identity. "Renaissance" denotes continuity of the tradition of the world literature as well as, paradoxically, liberation from the European past. New literature was to proclaim the revolutionary spirit of the new democratic culture and to show the way into the new era. The most prominent writers of the period are Emerson, Thoreau *Walden, Or Life in the Woods*, Whitman "Leaves of Grass", Dickinson, Poe, Hawthorne and Melville.

The mainstream literature was presented by romantic novels similar to chivalrous novels of Scott (frontier novel), those inspired by travels (travel novels; exotic), woman novels, sentimental novels. The romance developed to the typical genre of American literature. It allowed involvement of supernatural explanations and imaginative turns on the background of real historical events. Melville *Moby Dick,* Hawthorne *The Scarlet Letter*

1. Typical realism novel (*The Portrait of a Lady*)

The literature of the new period had to face the conflict between the rapid changes in the economic and social domains and the system of moral values and attitudes inherited from the Victorian England. Thus, literature was the testing ground for these conflicts.

Such conflicts were usually exposed in the encounters between representatives of different backgrounds, either geographical (North vs. South, Europe vs. America), or social (different walks of life). The prevailing patterns for such encounters were travels, love relationships, and social advancement and descent. The *Portrait* deals with all of these topics: it is an international novel comparing the Old and the New World, it is a story of courtship and marriage, and it treats relations between the English landowners, the American middle class, the rising American businessmen as well as all sorts of expatriates.

Howells *(The Rise of Silas Lapham* 1885)*,* James, Twain *(Adventures of Huckleberry Finn* 1885) saw the new American literature as a medium for writers and readers to participate in an active dialogue as to deficiencies of the new America. This is reflected in the new techniques, first of all, the reduction or even withdrawal of the omniscient narrating instance. The reader is compelled to make assumptions and to deduce the motivation behind the action. On the other hand, characters have ceased to represent types and their identity is not stable but developing within the novel, which leads to constant interpretation on part of the reader. To especially highlight the characterisation and development of characters the action is transferred from the outer events to the inner workings of the character. Reduction of (melo)dramatic occurrences takes place. The traditional happy ending is not always the case. Thus, the development of the American realistic novel displays an experiment where prefabricated interpretations done by the omniscient author are giving place to the reader's own conclusions.

Characteristics (from Richard Chase, *The American Novel and Its Tradition*)

1.   Renders reality closely and in comprehensive detail. Selective presentation of reality with an emphasis on verisimilitude, even at the expense of a well-made plot

2.   Character is more important than action and plot; complex ethical choices are often the subject.

3.   Characters appear in their real complexity of temperament and motive; they are in explicable relation to nature, to each other, to their social class, to their own past.

4.   Class is important; the novel has traditionally served the interests and aspirations of an insurgent middle class.

5.   Events will usually be plausible. Realistic novels avoid the sensational, dramatic

elements of naturalistic novels and romances.

6.   Diction is natural vernacular, not heightened or poetic; tone may be comic, satiric, or matter-of-fact.

7.   Objectivity in presentation becomes increasingly important: overt authorial comments or intrusions diminish as the century progresses.

8.   Interior or psychological realism a variant form.

The Portrait of a Lady (1881) is regarded a prototypical novel of American realism. The novel depicts a process of learning: a young unrefined American woman, Isabel Archer comes to Europe where she is exposed to different social and cultural influences, as well as gets wealthy, which helps her to get cultivated. Other characters are: Ralph Tuchett, an American living in England as landowner, Lord Warburton, a rich representative of the English gentry, Caspar Goodwood, a rich American industrialist, Gilbert Osmond, an American living as an outsider in Florence. This choice of characters allows for various opportunities, such as juxtapositions of assets and of backgrounds, conflicts, or love relationships. Other, minor characters are mostly Americans living in Europe, which allows for clashes as well. Thus the novel plays with different conflicting positions which were highly significant for the time of its appearance.

James himself admitted that the novel is a study of **character** – descriptive, analytic, psychological, concerned with fine shades and emotions. The most vivid example is the chapter where Isabel meditates before her fireplace on the disastrous failure of her marriage to Gilbert Osmond. James' famous characterisation in another chapter is a two-and-a-half-page paragraph where he gives an very discriminating exposition of Isabel's character. The novel is a study of **identity**, one pole is presented by Isabel Archer who expresses the view shared by James that there exists some essence of character. The other pole is expressed by Madame Merle who expands the materialist notion of identity suggesting a material shell around each person, "the whole envelope of circumstances", meaning that everything that belongs to a person expresses one's identity.

For Isabel her deep failure becomes an opportunity for **moral triumph**, as some critics suggest. The heroine inherits a fortune but does not turn materialistic and supercilious. Instead she undergoes moral chastening and recovers her original innocence but at a higher level. She does not let Caspar Goodwood lure herself with the promise of love and happiness but is eager to redeem her own mistake on the side of Osmond. For me personally, **the end of the novel** is very ambiguous. Does the return to Osmond mean her decision to accept consciously the role in which she found herself to be trapped? Or is it a flight from responsibilities of her own life without Osmond? Is it her own choice or is she merely driven by fear, an unconscious dread of sexuality?

The novel reflects typical features of American realism not only on the thematic level but also on the level of its structure and formal means. The omniscient 3rd person narrator allows an objective insight into various characters' minds, which is the hallmark of realism. Moreover, Isabel Archer as the character focaliser, is the centre of consciousness and her state of mind is given the utmost significance throughout the novel. The characters are complex psychological constructions involving much dynamic and development. The end of the novel is left open and in no case implies the happy ending.

There are certain questions concerning the structure of the novel. In the first place, is there a **plot**? The depiction of events seems more to be determined by the development of the main character than by a coherent plot behind them. James answers this concern in his Preface written 1908, 30 years after the novel first appeared. His theoretical focus lay on the developing of the character. The plot was not so important for his design.

Another question is whether the novel is **realistic** at all, since certain details considered significant for a realism novel are left out, e.g., Isabel's marriage, or the death of her baby.

However, for James, the value of fiction writing lay in providing "a personal, a direct impression of life," which to him was best achieved not by chronicling material conditions but rather by examining the subjective, psychological complexities of human beings.

James is mostly interested in the process which an American girl undergoes while freeing herself from the culturally imposed frame. This is also the case in *Daisy Miller* (1879) when a socially innocent and inexperienced young American woman behaves unconventionally while eager to gather experience prohibited in the society, thus becoming an outsider. In the end before she dies she opens up to the narrator who has failed to interpret her correctly.

Daisy Miller is the novel which brought James fame while he was still in his apprentice period. Already in this novel he introduced certain techniques, e.g., comparison between America and Europe, centre of consciousness (Winterbourne), psychological complexity of characters instead of reducing them to types, a novel as a study in psychology. Henry James's interest in psychology led him to develop the use of limited third-person narration, which is often regarded as one of his major contributions to American fiction. Limited 3rd person narration is a mode of narration that relies on narrators who are not omniscient but instead render descriptions and observations through the limitations of the central character. Readers must do more work - and involve themselves more in the process of meaning-making - to understand the relationship of the stories to their narration. This work is reflected in the predicaments of Winterbourne who establishes again and again a certain image of Daisy, but she defies his expectations every time.

Study – Winterbourne studies Daisy as Ralph studies Isabel and as the narrator of *Brooksmith* studies the butler. Focalisers are other persons, not the main characters. They give perspectives on the main characters.

2. Sophistication of realism novel (*The Wings of the Dove*).

The Wings of The Dove (1902) together with *The Golden Bowl* (1904) belong to the major phase and are quite different from other novels by James. All characters influence each other through constant changes of awareness and are thus in a permanent process of transformation which makes their identities very unstable. They reflect upon the behaviour of the others and, consequently, change their own behaviour. The positions of the manipulator and the manipulated are also changing.

The central characters, Kate Croy, Merton Densher and Milly Theale, are focalisers in Book I, II and III respectively. Thematically, the novel deals with subject typical for a realism novel. International theme - "Europe – the great American sedative"; Merton's experience in the USA; Kate, Aunt Maud, Lord Mark (London society, material interest, power, 'working' upon everybody) vs. Milly, Susan (USA, tradition); Americans exposed to Europeans and Europeans exposed to Americans. Class – only in London, mostly upper class, margin – Kate, her family, Merton. In the USA no class, mostly material differences. Pecuniary matters are very significant.

However, the novel is difficult to characterise as a merely realism novel, due to the formal feature it exploits. William James, Henry James' brother and a psychologist, remarked that in order to represent the characters' consciousness the story-telling was sacrificed.

The Wings of The Dove is a contradictory text. It tells the rather sordid, at times banal, and on the whole melodramatic **story** of a well-connected but penniless young Englishwoman, Kate Croy, who encourages her secret fiancé, Merton Densher, to pretend to fall in love with a wealthy but mortally stricken American heiress, Milly Theale, perhaps even to marry her, but in any case to put himself in a position to inherit some portion of her fabulous fortune. However, this story is told with large **gaps**: some very significant conversations take place between chapters; the crucial letter is thrown into the fire before anyone finds out what it says; the novel ends before the story is concluded. Despite its melodramatic plot, furthermore, the **language** is notoriously difficult, often undecidedly obscure: sentences wind interminably on, pronouns lack definite antecedents, characters use words like 'everything' and 'nothing' and phrases like "Well, there you are", which simultaneously suggest and obscure meanings and conclusions.

In short, the novel displays features of melodramatic realism together with those of modernism and postmodernism: it is **overtly melodramatic and textually evasive**. The reader has to read certain sentences and passages over and over again to make out the meaning and still remains baffled by the implications.

One of the glaring cases is the conversation between Milly and Sir Luke Strett, her doctor. On the level of story it is a highly significant moment in Milly's personal history; but on the level of plot it is an occasion for unaccustomed secrecy and deception as well as a melodramatic revelation. Although the chapter in question is large and much is said and much more is reflected upon, everything remains very vague – the kind of disease, in the first place. The conversation is reported in the most intense and yet the vaguest of terms, so that any understanding it conveys is both crucially important and totally inexplicit. This episode serves as a very apt example for the specific nature of James' works of his mature period. Milly's assessment of her condition is based on what she takes to be Sir Luke's 'pity' for her, she reads him, as she presumes, behind his mask. Neither he as doctor, nor she herself says anything definite about her condition.

However conventional this plot might be, the text blocks the reader's access to these conventional sequences, making "reading for the plot" frustrating and tedious. Reading the novel unsettles many historical, cultural, psychological assumptions of the reader. At the same time it is a challenge to read more actively. This is more so in Book III which displays voids and focuses even more intently on blanks (Merton's silence on his return from Venice, Milly's absence from London and lack of information on her state, her final letter is left unread and the rejection of her legacy open, the relationship between Kate and Merton has hollowed out). Eventually, the reader has to become a writer, in order to elaborate on the text and explore its possibilities.

In connection with the development of American realism, *The Wings of The Dove* can be seen as a further sophistication of its main principle, objectivity of representation, which demands a deep insight into the character's psyche. The acknowledged complexity of the psyche inevitably leads to ambivalence and obscurity of the character's motivations.

3. Elaboration of (American) realism novel.

The Art of Fiction (1884)

– critical essay on American novelists (Hawthorne)

– **the novel lacks theory**, reading was not seen as serious as painting, literature must get the same serious and aesthetic footing as painting has, it should be **art**, criticism helps fiction to turn important as art

– **novels should be good** – what is GOOD?: interesting – a direct impression of life, reality, experience, truth of detail; free – as long as the novel represents life; rich in topics, one does not have to write only about own experience, but have impressions...

– artist as observer of society

– realism – the supreme virtue

Preface to *The Portrait of a Lady* (1908)

- the architecture of his novels is built upon a single character (Isabel Archer)

- house of fiction – different windows – observer sees the same human scenery but everyone sees differently, how one sees depends on the 'literary form', 'the choice of subjects'

- window – frame, restriction, range: the artist should choose the subject since it is impossible to describe the whole life

- freedom to focus one's attention on the subject one chooses

- character – more important than the plot or story (Turgenieff, George Eliot); the germ of the novel is the consciousness of the single character, a character launches the story

- Isabel Archer is the centre of the novel, other characters are satellites; Isabel is always in 'the coach', others – only for a period of time

Preface to *The Wings of The Dove* (1908)

- blocks (7) – successive centres, 'communities of doom', 'a big vessel'

- Milly = Lorelei, draws Kate and Merton in the abysmal trap, whirlpool, by imposing complications on them; characters are deeply affected by the encounter with Milly, Milly is doomed and the successful centre (Kate + Merton) goes down too

- the outward outcome is satisfying but the inward result is not, the 'villains' succeed but they cannot enjoy it

- Mrs. Stringham is a supplementary reflector, connecting link, interpreter

Does the preface describe the novel accurately? - revision, elucidation